A Nature Guide to the

Ardara Portnoo

Area of County Donegal

A Nature Guide to the
Ardara Portnoo
Area of County Donegal

RICHARD NAIRN

First published in 2007 by
The Nature Press
Broomhall Business Park
Rathnew
Co. Wicklow
Ireland
www.naturepress.ie

British Library Cataloguing in Publication Data

Nairn, Richard, 1952-
A Nature Guide to the Ardara Portnoo Area of County Donegal

ISBN 978-0-9556328-0-8

Design and layout by Anú Design, Tara, Co. Meath
Printed in Ireland by Ruon Print, Rathnew, Co. Wicklow

This publication has received support from the Heritage Council under the 2007 Publications Grant Scheme.

Contents

Preface

Natural History is an old-fashioned term. As a scientific pursuit it was born in the 18th century and some believe it reached its zenith in the late 19th century with naturalists like Charles Darwin and, in Ireland, Robert Lloyd Praeger. But natural history is still alive and well today, although now we more often call it ecology or environmental science. It is the study of nature in all its amazing forms and functions. There are few more satisfying endeavours in natural history than to look in detail at the ecology of one small area, trying to relate its plants and animals to the habitats, geology and land use.

Praeger was the leader of a band of naturalists who studied the island of Lambay, off Dublin, and he published their findings in 1907, exactly one hundred years ago. In his autobiography, *The Way that I Went*, he wrote: "It was the unexpected success of this intensive study of a limited area that led to the carrying out a few years later of a similar undertaking on a much larger scale – the Clare Island Survey, which added very largely to our knowledge of the fauna and flora of Ireland."

This area around Ardara and Portnoo, in County Donegal, is one of a few spots in Ireland which offer the naturalist almost endless possibilities. At its core is a rich diversity of natural habitats, which yields an equally rich harvest of species in whatever group one chooses to study. I have been fortunate, like the conductor of an orchestra, to have had the cooperation of many fine players, each one an expert in their own fields. When brought together, they produce a symphony of nature. The same could easily be achieved for many other such areas.

Acknowledgements

The Heritage Council is acknowledged for its support of this book through its Publications Grants Scheme. The book is also part-funded by Donegal County Council under the County Donegal Heritage Plan (2007–2011).

I am very grateful to a number of scientists and naturalists who have given freely of their knowledge and records to add to the interest of this publication. The following people wrote sections of the text: Bob Aldwell on butterflies, Dr David Cabot on H.C. Hart, John Cromie on moths, Dr Julie Fossitt on vegetation history, Dr Andrew Large on geology and geomorphology, Stephen McCormack on beetles, Dr Evelyn Moorkens on molluscs, Dr Brian Nelson on dragonflies, and Ralph Sheppard on plants. Others, who contributed in a variety of ways, were: Dr Roy Anderson, Una Brown, John Hennigan, Emer Magee, Patrick and Jill Moss, Dr Andy Sleeman and Mike Trewby. The general maps were expertly prepared by Ciara Hamilton. The geological map is reproduced with permission of the Geological Survey of Ireland. Photographs were supplied by Dr Roy Anderson, Andrew Kelly, Dr Evelyn Moorkens, Mike Trewby and Robert Thompson, each of whom is credited under their pictures. All other photographs are by the author. The text was kindly edited by Dr Karl Partridge and Juanita Browne. Michael Longley generously allowed me to quote from his poem *Spring Tide*, by permission of the publishers, Jonathan Cape. Layout and design were by Karen Carty and Terry Foley of Anú Design. I am indebted to Brian and Olivia Farrington for the use, over many years, of their house at Rosbeg, as a base to explore the area. I owe much to my wife, Wendy, who enjoys exploring this area as much as I do. The book is dedicated to Michael Viney, Ireland's finest natural history writer, and a special friend.

Richard Nairn
June 2007

The zig-zags I make take me among
White cresses and brookweed, lousewort,
Water plantain and grass of parnassus,
With engraved capillaries, ivory sheen:
By a dry stone wall in the dune slack
The greenish sepals, the hidden blush
And a lip's red veins and yellow spots –
Marsh helleborine waiting for me
To come and go with the spring tide.

From *Spring Tide* by Michael Longley

Opposite: Marsh Helleborine

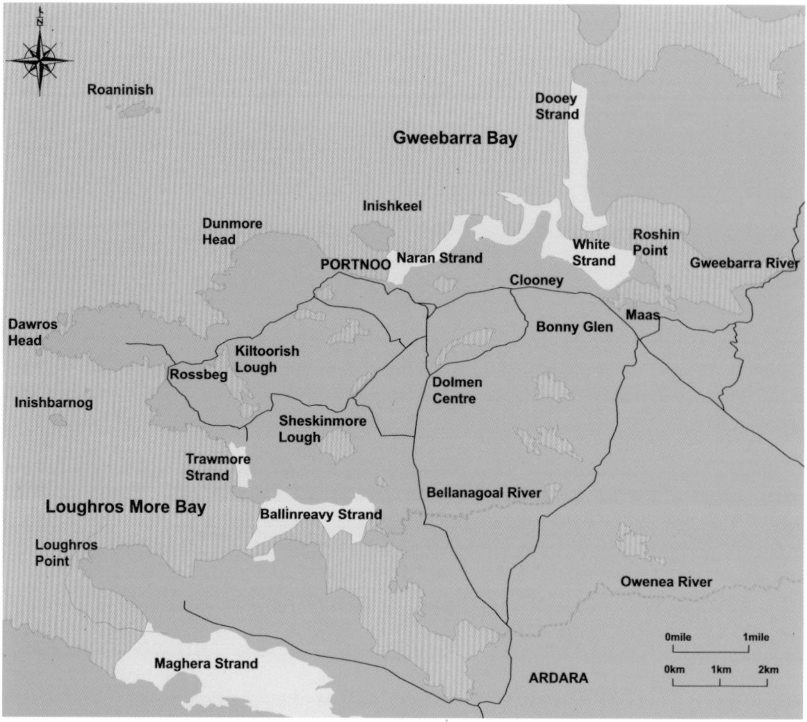
Roaninish
Dooey Strand
Gweebarra Bay
Inishkeel
Dunmore Head
Roshin Point
White Strand
PORTNOO
Naran Strand
Gweebarra River
Clooney
Dawros Head
Maas
Bonny Glen
Kiltoorish Lough
Rossbeg
Dolmen Centre
Inishbarnog
Sheskinmore Lough
Trawmore Strand
Bellanagoal River
Loughros More Bay
Ballinreavy Strand
Loughros Point
Owenea River
0mile
1mile
Maghera Strand
0km
1km
2km
ARDARA

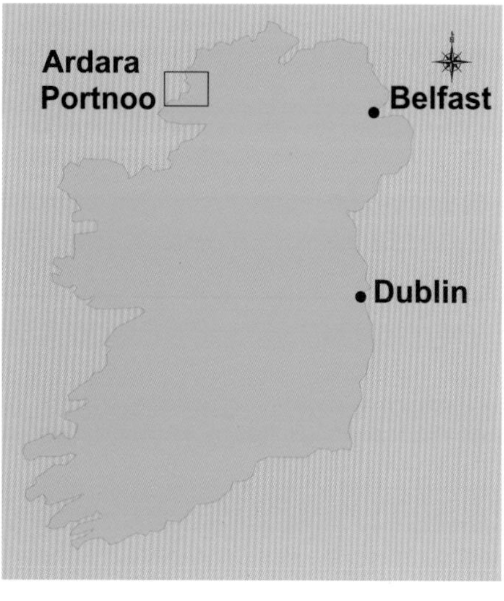
Ardara Portnoo
Belfast
Dublin

Introduction

The famous naturalist, Robert Lloyd Praeger wrote in 1937 of "the wild Dawros promontory, not lofty, but full of little heathery hills and lakes, with a sandy or cliffy shore – a particularly attractive area". This description is still true today some seventy years later. This guide is intended as an introduction to the wildlife and natural features of the Ardara-Portnoo area on the west coast of Donegal. Despite its small size, this area is rich and diverse in rock types, habitats and species. This short account can only scrape the surface of the landscape but it may help the reader to explore the area and discover its natural history. Some aspects of the natural environment have been well recorded but others still remain to be uncovered. The more the area is studied, the more interesting and unique features are likely to be revealed. The archaeology and human history of the area are explored in Lochlainn McGill's book, *In Conal's Footsteps* (2001).

This account mainly covers the triangular area of land between the coast and the R261 road from Maas to Ardara. It measures approximately 10km by 10km. Its most westerly point is Dawros (from *Damh Ros* meaning headland of the oxen). Almost all of the area is designated as a Special Area of Conservation, which is the highest level of protection available in Europe. Some parts are also designated as a Special Protection Area for birds (mainly the chough). The estuaries of Gweebarra to the north, Loughros More and Loughros Beg to the south, are also included. The whole area offers the naturalist a wide range of landscapes, rock formations, habitats, flora and fauna in both the marine and terrestrial environments. Due to its location on the edge of the Atlantic Ocean, it is a pristine, largely unpolluted environment. The town of Ardara makes an ideal base from which to explore the natural history of the region. A list of places to visit is given at the back of this book.

Kelp drying wall at Rossbeg (top); Folded Dalradian Schist at Maghara (bottom)

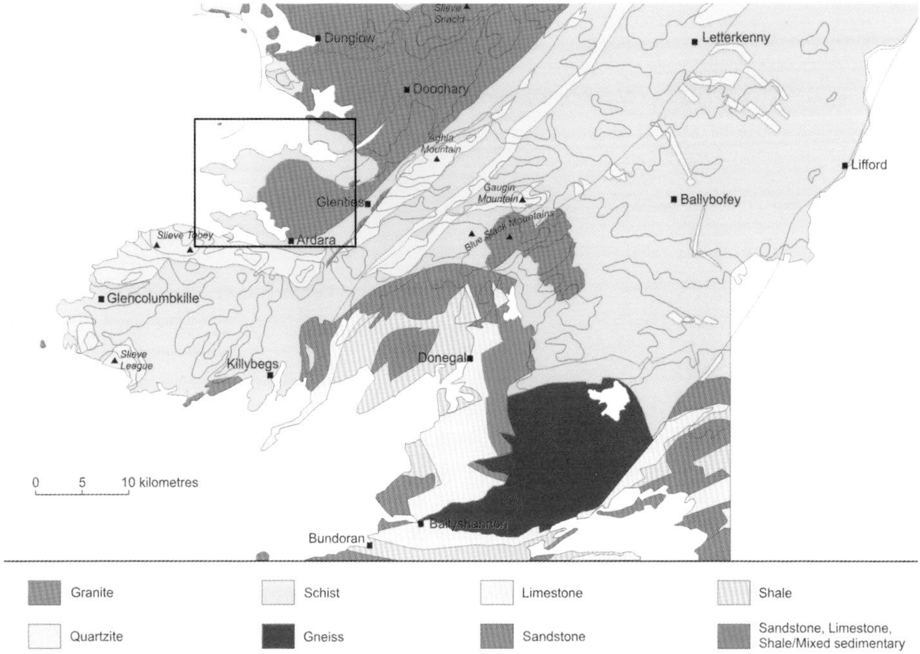

Simplified geological map of South Donegal. The rectangle indicates the Ardara-Portnoo area *(courtesy of the Geological Survey of Ireland)*

Geology

The rocks of the Ardara-Portnoo area are varied and complex, so much so that Donegal was the last county in Ireland to be geologically mapped. The peninsula is situated on an area of ancient Dalradian schist dating back to around 600 million years ago for southwest Donegal. This is a type of rock known as *metamorphic* that has been altered by heat and pressure (usually due to volcanic activity or earth movements). In this case the schist originated as mudstones and sandstones deposited due to earlier deformation of the earth's crust. In the Ardara-Portnoo region, it is usually formed into flat sheets that are easily broken into stones for building. These flagstones can be seen in the region's many stone walls and traditional buildings, such as barns. The schist is from a type known as the Upper Falcarragh Pelite formation, which was first described from the north Donegal coast.

The metamorphic schist forms the envelope (country rock) around an almost circular intrusion of *igneous* rock known as the Ardara Pluton, the edge of which forms the eastern side of Sheskinmore Lough. Igneous rocks are those formed as molten magma deep in the earth's crust and emerge either explosively (as a volcanic eruption) or slowly (by erosion of the overlying layers). In this case, the granite emerged slowly over millions of years. The granites were initially emplaced as a result of extensive tectonic activity at continental margins between 420-400 million years ago. At this time the position of the Earth's surface, currently occupied by modern Ireland, was extremely dynamic (being at a diverging or speading point between ancient continents). Donegal occupies the point where the future Atlantic Ocean was born. The Ardara granite can be envisaged in 3-D form as a balloon-shaped mass of granite, which cooled slowly over millions of years thus allowing the characteristic crystals of quartz, feldspar and mica to form. There were five main episodes

Cave and rockfall at Maghera

of granite emplacement over a 20 million year period at approximate depths of 10km in the earth's crust (the implication is that this 10km of crust has disappeared by erosion over the intervening period). Different granite bodies differ in colour due to the chemical composition of their feldspars, so the granites west of Ardara differ from those of the Trawenagh and Rosses granites to the north of the Gweebarra estuary at Lettermacaward.

Along the shore between Naran and Portnoo, and on Dunmore Head, is an area of crystalline limestone. This was originally a *sedimentary* rock, which means that it was laid down millions of years ago on the bed of a shallow sea although it has since been altered by the heat from later earth movements. Limestone is a relatively soft rock and is easily eroded by the sea or by rainfall, producing some interesting natural sculptures. The crevices in the limestone are also used today by marine animals living in the rock pools. The limestones form part of the Lower Falcarragh Succession, and therefore significantly pre-date the Carboniferous limestones so characteristic of other parts of Ireland. In places (for example directly to the west of Portnoo harbour), they are finely folded and thus are beautifully metamorphosed.

Glaciation

During the last Ice Age the area was covered with thick ice sheets. These left behind a number of *stria* (or scratch marks on the rocks) which show the direction in which the glaciers moved. The ice carried with it a large amount of sand and gravel, eroded further inland, and this was deposited after the glaciers melted forming the distinctive drumlins (small rounded hills) and other deposition features. The last glacial maximum was about 15,000 years ago with a small advance recorded in places dating to between 11-10,000 years ago. Glaciers completely reshaped and denuded the landscape and reformed the surface topography and drainage. In the Ardara-Portnoo area, superb examples of U-shaped valleys include Glengesh and Granny Glen, near Maghera. These valleys normally follow pre-existing geological faultlines where the ice could preferentallly scour the crushed and weakened rocks of the Earth's crust. After the ice retreated the area was affected by sea level change due to icemelt and crustal rise (isostatic rebound) once the heavy mantle of ice was removed. Overall, the Irish coastline is still rising since the great weight of the glaciers was removed. Post-glacial fluctuations in sea level are demonstrated by the presence of peat among the beach stones around Rossbeg.

Wood sage growing in a stone wall

Vegetation History

Pollen grains and other material that accumulate at the bottom of lakes tell the story of a region's changing vegetation and environment over time. Analyses of cores from three small lakes in western Donegal, one on the Loughros peninsula and two in the Rosses, revealed records that extended back to the end of the Ice Age. The late-glacial landscape was characterised by open tundra vegetation, dominated by herb-rich grasslands, with phases of crowberry heath or juniper scrub expansion depending on climatic conditions, and possibly also grazing levels as populations of reindeer and the now extinct giant Irish elk fluctuated. About 11,000 years ago, the climate warmed sufficiently to allow the expansion of trees. The early woodlands were dominated by birch and hazel. Diversity increased as oak, elm, Scots pine and, later, alder migrated into the area. Mixed woodland developed and dominated the landscape 9000 years ago but was more open in the Rosses than further south. The first real signs of disturbance linked with human activity and the start of farming became evident about 6000 years ago. Tree populations fluctuated initially and yew and ash invaded as elm declined and Scots pine underwent a short-lived expansion. The many pine stumps that can be seen in bogs today bear witness to its demise. The general trend over the last 5000 years was a gradual but progressive woodland decline as bog, heath and grassland expanded. Western Donegal had become an open, largely treeless area 2000 years ago. A full account of the paleoecology of this area is given in a paper by Fossitt, J.A. 1994. Late-glacial and Holocene vegetation history of western Donegal, Ireland. *Biology and Environment: Proceedings of the Royal Irish Academy* 94B, 1-31.

Dune slack and sand dunes at Trawmore

In Loughros Beg Bay, on the north side of Maghera Strand, there are fossil sand dunes that have been buried by blanket bog. A sample, taken from the bog here by Frank Mitchell, gave an age of 4,200 years before present. This is one of the earliest dates known in Ireland for blanket bog formation and also indicates a climatic change which caused the dunes to become waterlogged and peat to form.

Further information on the geology and archaeology of the area is available at the Dolmen Centre at Kilclooney on the R261 road between Naran and Ardara. This is well worth a visit with opening hours between 11am and 4pm in summer time.

Habitats

The habitats in the area today are a mixture of marine, coastal, land and freshwater ecosystems which are diverse and largely unspoilt. To describe the habitats we use standard terms from *A Guide to Habitats in Ireland*, published by the Heritage Council (Fossitt 2000). This helps naturalists to compare such habitats with similar features elsewhere.

Land and Freshwater Habitats

Freshwater lakes: In the area between Portnoo and Ardara, there is a scattering of small lakes in the hollows between the hills. These are mainly surrounded by heathy ground but some have small patches of reeds in the shallower waters. The lake at Sheskinmore is shallow with a sandy bed. It is surrounded by a dense reedswamp. The water here is alkaline and contains several submerged plants. Clooney Lough is also alkaline as its outlet is blocked by sand dunes. Kiltoorish Lough near Rosbeg is also shallow with a sandy bed near the southern end where it is bordered by sand dunes. The northern end has a rocky shoreline and reedswamp. The sandy beds of several of the loughs in the locality reflects either their past development as lagoon features subsequently cut-off from the sea by dune formation (e.g. Sheskinmore) or the influx of sand though aeolian (wind) erosion and transport.

Heath: The rocky habitats, which are common everywhere between Dawros Head and the R261 road, are frequently covered with heathland. This is dominated by heathers, with juniper as a common component. Dry siliceous heath is the commonest type but wet heath is also present where the drainage is poor. A typical plant of wet heath is cross-leaved heath.

Reedswamp (left) and juniper heath

Grasslands: Many of the grasslands of the area are unimproved although lightly grazed by sheep or cattle. The grasslands within Sheskinmore nature reserve are some of the finest dry calcareous grasslands in Ireland with a rich variety of flora in summer. These grade into marsh which is constantly wet underfoot. It is distinguished by the dominance of herbs such as water mint and bogbean. Some of the fields in the area are used for hay-making and are classed as dry meadows. These tend to have a richer flora as they are often not mown till late summer. There is dry humid acid grassland in between the areas of heath. Wet grassland occurs in some of the hollows with rushes and sedges dominant. Improved agricultural grassland is found in places where fertilising and reseeding has occurred.

Bogs: The inland area between Portnoo and Ardara has some areas of lowland blanket bog. This vegetation occurs where the peat is a little deeper and the plants gain most of their moisture from the rain. Important plants here are the bog mosses (*Sphagnum* species) which contribute to the formation of peat and indicate that the bog is growing and in a relatively healthy condition.

Woodland and scrub: The surviving woodlands in the area are small fragments of the original tree cover. There is a good area of mixed broad-leaved woodland at the northern end of Kiltoorish Lough around Eden House. This has a mix of trees including ash, oak and sycamore. There is a sizeable stand of native woodland at Bonny Glen, south of Clooney, which is dominated by oak and birch. A steep woodland of hazel occurs just above the shoreline of White Strand, north of Clooney.

Other small patches of woodland survive on steep rocky cliffs, such as that at the western side of Kiltoorish Lough and on the slopes north of Sheskinmore Lough. Around Summy Lough and Lough Fad there are two areas of semi-natural woodland which comprise mainly sessile oak and there are areas of hazel scrub around Doon Lough, Clooney Lough and Lough Dowen. Hazel was once widely used for the production of pliable rods which had many uses, including the making of lobster pots. Scrub, mainly gorse and bramble, is present in a few areas.

Exposed rock: Rocky ground is common in the area. The sea cliffs at Dawros Head and Dunmore Head provide some dramatic scenery. Lichens are among the few plants that can grow on these habitats and are abundant. Exposed rock is also found on some inland cliffs such as those along the road from Portnoo to Rosbeg.

Clockwise from top: Calcareous grassland; oak woodland; and blanket bog

Sand dunes: Gweebarra Bay and Loughros More Bay contain some extensive sand dune habitats. These include the dunes of Trawmore and Sheskinmore on Loughros More Bay and the Naran Beach to White Strand area on the south side of Gweebarra Bay. Dooey Dunes, north of Gweebarra, are also important. At Trawmore, the dunes have been growing towards the sea at a very rapid rate since about 1990. The marram grass traps the blowing sand off the beach and forms small embryo dunes on the beach. Behind these are low wet areas called dune slacks, with a mixture of coastal and wetland plants. In Neolithic times (around 4,500 years ago), these dune systems were utilised by nomadic communities who used the coast in summer time for fishing and grazing. Remains of their activities can be seen as kitchen middens, comprising layers of shell and burnt stones used for cooking buried within the white quartzite sands of the exposed dune faces.

The modern day high sand dune systems were probably formed in the Medieval period, or earlier, and are largely covered in marram grass. These are very extensive and have a number of wet dune slacks in the low-lying hollows between. On the south side of Gweebarra Bay a series of dune systems have formed between Naran and Maas. These have been partly modified by a caravan park and golf links. Trawmore near Rossbeg is an interesting example of a healthy beach system fed by longshore drift of sand from the eroding Ballinreavy strand to the east (separated from Trawmore by the rocky point of Carrickalahagh), Trawmore itself is rapidly accumulating sand with embryo dunes interspersed with flower-rich wet slack systems. Elsewhere, at Naran, concern about dune erosion in the locality of the golf course has resulted in artificial efforts to halt or slow this inevitable process.

Machair: Behind the sand dunes at Sheskinmore, an area of flat dune grassland has formed as a result of grazing. This is a distinctive type of grassland known as *machair*, which is unique in Europe and found only in western Ireland and Scotland. These grasslands are sandy, calcareous (lime-rich) and have very diverse plant communities. In summer, the machair is covered with wild flowers including orchids and grass-of-parnassis. There is also some machair at Dooey, north of Gweebarra. These plant communities are of prime conservation

Opposite: Embryo sand dunes at Trawmore

Machair and marsh at Sheskinmore

importance, yet current monitoring of the eroding Ballinreavy dune system directly to the south shows that the dune system could breach in a period of anywhere from 15 to 40 years, potentially impacting these delicate and valuable habitats and the allied fen-lake complex.

Saltmarsh: Between Clooney and Maas, there is an extensive area of saltmarsh fringing the Black Strand. This is ungrazed and is dominated by saltmarsh rushes. There is also a large area of saltmarsh at the mouth of the Ballinagoal River, midway between Rosbeg and Ardara. This area was grazed by sheep and part of it was used as a football pitch, but it is now a protected area. Saltmarsh is covered only by high spring tides.

Shingle Beaches: Many of the more exposed beaches between Portnoo and Rosbeg have large shingle or cobble banks thrown up by winter storms. These have some typical shingle plants such as sea beet and oraches. The strandline on these beaches is often covered in a thick bed of wrack (or stranded brown seaweeds). This rots down and provides an ideal growing medium for the few annual plants that can survive here. Some of the beaches have exposed peat among the stones which shows that the sea level here was much lower thousands of years ago.

Saltmarsh (left) and shingle beach

Marine Habitats

Rocky Shores: The majority of the shorelines between Portnoo and Rosbeg are rocky with good examples around Dawros Head and Inishkeel. In the latter case, the rock is limestone which provides many more pools and crevices for intertidal creatures. The seaweeds on these rocky shores are arranged in zones from low tide mark to high tide mark and the species vary according to the degree of exposure. The dominant shellfish on the most exposed shorelines are encrusting barnacles and mussels. Periwinkles are also common in crevices and under stones.

Sandy Shores: The shorelines of medium exposure, where the sea is depositing sediment, form sandy beaches. The best examples are at Trawmore and Ballinreavy Strand on Loughros More Bay and between Narin Beach and White Strand on Gweebarra Bay. Maghara Strand in Loughros Beg Bay also has a very large area of sandy beach. Although they often appear quite barren, sandy beaches have a distinctive fauna which lives buried beneath the surface. This includes cockles, razorshells and the heart urchin.

Islands

The largest island in the area is Inishkeel, off Portnoo, although this is connected to the mainland by a sand bar at low tide. This became an important religious centre in the 6th century AD and by the 18th century a Turas or pilgrim's walk had been established here. The last family to live on the island moved to the mainland in 1904, but their abandoned farmhouse can still be seen. Also on the eastern (sheltered) end of the island there are the remains of two churches and a graveyard with some interesting grave slabs. The island is grazed by barnacle geese in winter and a few gulls breed in summer.

About 6km north-west of Portnoo is the tiny flat island of Roaninish, named after the seals that haul out here. It also has breeding eider duck, storm petrel and occasional tern colonies. In calm weather it is just possible to land in a small bay on the east side of the island. There is a small lake on the island and sheep are put out to graze here in summer. In 1952 a large ship ran aground on the island but the crew were rescued by helicopter in one of the first air-sea rescue missions in Ireland.

The third island in the area is Inishbarnog, lying due south of Dawros Head. It has a small sandy beach on the east side, facing Rosbeg, where landing is possible in a small boat. Sheep also graze this island in summer and barnacle geese use it in winter. Herring gulls and oystercatcher breed here. In the mouth of Gweebarra River estuary there is a string of small islets, many with grassy tops. These are used by the harbour seals for hauling out at low tide. These islands are also important as they offer safe high-tide roosting sites for wading birds such as oystercatcher and curlew and 'lying up' places for the otter.

Clockwise from top: Mussels; lugworm; casts; Naran Strand

Inishkeel island forms a tombolo or arctuate spit of sand connecting the island to the mainland (in a world-wide context these are unusual among beach-related landforms as the islands protecting them are short-lived in a geological sense).

Muddy Shores: In the most sheltered areas of the coast fine mud is deposited forming soft mudflats. This habitat is well represented at the Black Strand, north of Maas, and in the inner Loughros More Bay near Ardara. Here the invertebrate fauna is rich and attracts flocks of waders in winter. The mud surface is often covered by green algae and may have colonising saltmarsh plants. Typical marine fauna of the muddy areas includes lugworm, ragworm and tiny marine snails called *Hydrobia.*

Flora and Fauna Checklists

The flora and fauna of the Ardara-Portnoo area has been relatively well studied compared with similar areas on the west coast of Ireland. Even so, we know very little about certain groups such as bats, mosses, lichens, fish, and marine fauna generally. The following accounts are brief summaries of what is currently known. Species mentioned in the text are listed at the back of the book together with their scientific names. These can be used as checklists or simply as a starting point for naturalists who want to discover more. A short list of good field identification guides is given at the back of this book.

Flora

Praeger wrote in 1937, "Below the scattered line of houses of Portnoo, green fields, white with pignut instead of daisies, slope steeply to a rocky shore". The Ardara- Portnoo area is still an excellent place to see a wide range of native plants in a relatively small area. This is because of the close proximity of a great variety of habitats, the interaction of land and sea and the low intensity of land use found here. Even a short walk in a local field or woodland will produce a rich assortment of flowering plants, mosses and lichens. The range of common grasses in some of the meadows is quite striking. Heathland and dune plants are especially well represented in this area.

H.C. Hart, Botanist

Henry Chichester Hart (1847-1908) was the leading authority of his time on the flora of Co. Donegal. His family was from Donegal although he was born in Dublin where his father was Vice-Provost of Trinity College. Hart began his exploration of the botany of Donegal at the age of seventeen and in 1898 published his *Flora of the County Donegal*. This is now a very rare volume as most copies of the book were destroyed by fire during the 1916 Rising. Most of the plant records in the Flora came from Hart's own personal observations - he traversed the County like a colossus recording all he saw. The Ardara-Portnoo area fell within the Barony of Boylagh. One species of note that he found here was the bog cotton *Eriophorum latifolium*. It was a very rare plant in Donegal at the time when first found by Hart in 1886. It was lurking in a low marshy pasture at Sheskinmore Lough. Hart also recorded, in the same year, the deadly nightshade *Atropa belladonna* growing on the rocky limestone coast, east of Inishkeel Island. Hart believed that it was native here while Praeger later wrote in his *The Botanist in Ireland* (1934) that it had been naturalised.

According to Praeger (1949), Hart was "a man of magnificent physique, a daring climber and tireless walker. He missed little and penetrated to places where few have followed him". When out botanising in the hills and mountains most of his companions were unable to keep up with him and were often left behind. That is why most of his botanising was done alone. As a bet he once walked from Dublin to the summit of Lugnaquilla, Co. Wicklow, – about 40km away – and back again within 24 hours. He was also totally indifferent to weather conditions.

In 1875, Hart was appointed as naturalist on HMS Discovery joining a polar expedition and he subsequently published the results as *Botany of the British Polar Expedition* 1975-6. He also participated in an expedition to explore the geological structure of the Jordan Valley and Western Palestine in 1883. Hart later published three reports on the Flora of Palestine. His interests extended well beyond natural history. His knowledge of Elizabethan literature was remarkable and he edited many of Shakespeare's plays as well as publishing Scripture Natural History: *The Animals mentioned in the Bible* (1888). He is buried at Glenalla, set in beautiful surroundings and close to the Hart ancestral home in Donegal.

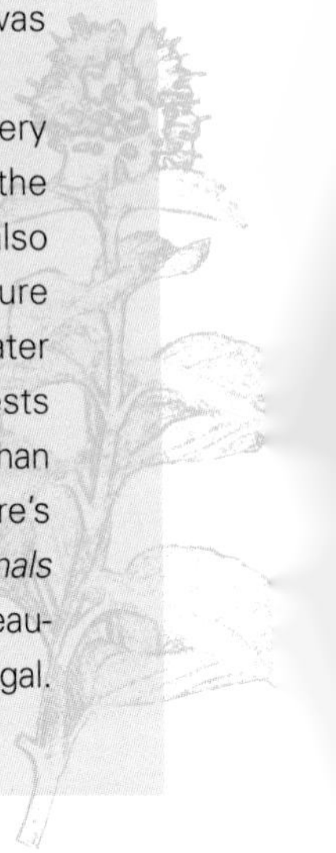

Some of the key plant species are mentioned under the habitat accounts above. Rare species are also known from these habitats although the area is probably under-recorded in this respect. Sheskinmore is probably the best area for finding rare plant species as it has a wide range of semi-natural habitat types in close proximity and is managed as a nature reserve to maximise biodiversity. The rarest species is a submerged aquatic plant, called the slender naiad, which is found in Sheskinmore Lough, Clooney Lough and Kiltooris Lough. The damp sandy grasslands around Sheskinmore hold a wide variety of orchids including several rare varieties of the marsh orchid. This is also the most northerly site known in Ireland for the Irish dense-flowered orchid. Near their southern limit are arctic species like hoary whitlowgrass and bearberry.

Other rare plants include the bee orchid, a few of which are seen in most years, and the beautiful marsh helleborine which grows in large numbers in the wet machair. Heath cudweed is a rapidly declining species. Pipewort from

Opposite: Grass-of-Parnassus

Clockwise from top: Hareball; marsh orchid; water mint

North America, and quillwort, which is a relative of the ferns, are found in lakes. In the dunes, is found a relative of the mosses, called petalwort, which is rare throughout Europe. In fens the greater spearwort has been found.

Just as important as the rare plants is the abundance of so many of the common wildflowers, from wild thyme, bulbous buttercup and heath dog-violet in the sandy habitats, meadow thistle, devil's-bit scabious and sheep's-bit on the heathy ground, to primroses, harebells and bluebells almost anywhere. This abundance and diversity of common plants is increasingly rare in the modern landscape. Seventy years ago, Praeger (1937) noted the lateness of the growing season here. "In early June it is still spring; the slope to the sea is full of primroses, wild hyacinths and even wood anemones; and in the little lakes the water lobelia and American pipewort are yet hardly stirring".

Clockwise from top left: Ragged robin; black bog rush; knapweed; common clubrush

Seaweeds

Few flowering plants occur below high water mark but their place is taken by the seaweeds or marine algae. Although they may all look superficially similar, seaweeds comprise a variety of species, each one adapted to the environmental conditions in which they are found. The different seaweeds provide valuable shelter and food for many marine animals. Seaweeds come in a huge variety of sizes, shapes and colours (brown, green, red and occasionally yellow). The larger species include the kelps, which form tall "forests" near low water mark. Each plant or stem has a massive holdfast, which attaches it to rocks or large stones. Sometimes, after storms, these are torn loose from the seabed and washed up on beaches. The typical brown seaweeds that blanket much of the rocky shores in this area are arranged in horizontal zones, parallel to the tideline. The occurrence of each species is related to the degree of exposure to waves. The main species are bladder wrack, serrated wrack and spiral wrack. These formed the main ingredient of the kelp burnt in previous centuries to produce lime. In more sheltered areas and in the rock pools that are exposed at low tide, some fine leaved red and green seaweeds occur. The presence of an abundance of *Enteromorpha* can indicate enriched water, such as where a freshwater stream emerges on the shore. Some seaweeds can be eaten, and these include a traditional food called dulse or dilisc, which was collected at low tide and dried in the sun.

Opposite: Bladder wrack and spiral wrack near Rossbeg Pier

Fauna

Land Mammals: Larger land mammals such as deer are generally absent from the area but fox and badger are fairly widespread. In the absence of extensive woodland and scrub, badgers will dig their setts in open ground, including sand dunes. Foxes are often seen by day hunting rabbits in the dunes. Otter occur widely in the area as shown by their droppings or spraints. They feed extensively on shoreline animals such as crabs, shellfish and rocky shore fish. They can be seen by day in some of the more remote areas such as Rosheen Point, Dawros Head and around Loughros More Bay. The introduced American mink is also present in the area as there was a mink farm close to Glenties for many years and some animals escaped to live in the wild. The stoat is common especially in dune areas where its main prey the rabbit is concentrated. The pine martin has recently spread back to the area and has been recorded at Clooney Wood but the general scarcity of its woodland habitat suggests that it will never be common here. Mountain hares are often seen on some of the fields and bogs, as well as on the island of Inishkeel. Smaller mammals such

Otter eating a shorefish *(Éamon de Buitléar)*

Grey seal

rats, mice, shrews and hedgehogs are probably common but are rarely seen because they are mainly nocturnal. Bats are active during the summer months and prefer to feed around wooded areas such as Bonny Glen or at the northern end of Kiltoorish Lough.

Marine Mammals: Both grey seal and harbour (common) seal can be seen at the mouth of Gweebarra Estuary. The harbour seals breeding here number at least 50 animals and around 10 pups are born in June-July. They have finely spotted coats and can swim immediately after birth. A few grey seals can often be seen among the harbour seals at haul-out sites. Grey seals breed in caves and storm beaches beneath the cliffs at Slievetooey to the south of Loughros More Bay. Occasionally, a white-coated pup may be washed up on the shores around Rosbeg in the autumn months. Whales and dolphins are probably fairly frequent visitors to these waters during the summer months. The large and impressive killer whale has been seen by local fishermen in the area south of Dawros Head. Recent sightings include harbour porpoise in Gweebarra Bay and Loughros More Bay and bottlenosed dolphin off Portnoo. Recently stranded cetaceans in this area include harbour porpoise, bottlenosed dolphin, striped dolphin and minke whale (for more information see the website www.iwdg.ie).

Leathery turtle at Rossbeg Pier 1983

Reptiles and Amphibians: The leathery turtle, a large marine reptile, migrates into Irish waters in summer and is sometimes found in Loughros More Bay. One of these huge animals became tangled in fishing gear in 1983 and was landed at the pier in Rosbeg. The only land reptile in Ireland, the common lizard, is found in the sand dunes around the area and often basks on rocks in the sun. The common frog is found in many freshwater habitats and the common newt is also present.

Summer birds: The summer birds around Ardara-Portnoo are typical of much of the north-west coast of Ireland. Common birds of prey include kestrel, breeding on Dawros Head and sparrowhawk in the woodlands at Bonny Glen and Kiltoorish Lough. A pair of peregrine falcon breeds on cliffs and can be seen hunting almost anywhere in the area. Over the next few years there is a good chance of seeing golden eagle hunting in the this area as some of the young eagles released in Glenveagh National Park – as part of the Golden

Eagle Reintroduction Project – havc been seen around the cliffs of Slievetooey, south west of Loughros Beg Bay.

Choughs are resident in the area with pairs breeding at Dunmore Head and occasionally at Dawros Head and flocks feeding especially in the dunes at Sheskinmore. Historically, choughs bred in the church on Inishkeel and some of the gravestones here are engraved with birds resembling choughs.

Ravens are breed on the cliffs and rocky areas and constantly patrol the area in search of carrion to scavenge. Among the waders, ringed plover breed on Trawmore and on the beaches around Gweebarra Bay. Common sandpiper breed around Kiltoorish Lough and Sheskinmore Lough. Other breeding waders found here are oystercatcher, lapwing and snipe.

Typical small birds are stonechat, wheatear and rock pipit on the more exposed coastal areas with linnet, willow warbler and reed bunting where there is more scrub cover. Meadow pipit and skylark are common in the sand dunes and on bogs. The meadow pipit is the main host of the cuckoo, a summer visitor to the area. The woodland areas hold a typical community of songbirds dominated by chaffinch, robin, wren, blackbird, great tit and blue tit. In late summer, the area is alive with large flocks of starling which feed in the sandy

Dunlin on a shingle shore

Clockwise from left: Chough *(Andrew Kelly)*, sanderling, barnacle goose

areas and roost at night in scrub or reedbeds. The fringes of wetlands, such as Sheskinmore, Clooney and Kiltoorish Loughs, are used by breeding mallard, sedge warbler and reed bunting. Grey herons are commonly seen feeding on the coastline, lakeshores, streams and marshes.

Seabirds breed in small colonies on Roaninish, Inishbarnog and Dawros Head. These include gulls and terns with a few pairs of shag and black guillemot. Eider duck also breed on Roaninish and can be seen later in the summer feeding in the surf on the mainland bays. Also breeding in the islands are cormorant, storm petrel, arctic tern, herring gull, great black backed gull and common gull. Other seabirds such as fulmar, gannet, guillemot and razorbill are frequently seen fishing in the bays in summer. Dawros Head is a good location for sea-watching, especially at migration time and during onshore winds, when passing seabirds are driven close inshore.

Winter birds: In winter the area is a destination for a number of migrant birds. Of particular interest are the geese and swans. A flock of Greenland white-fronted geese regularly winters at Sheskinmore Lough. The white-fronts also use some of the bog lakes inland. Barnacle geese are frequently seen on the islands of Inishkeel, Roaninish and Inishbarnog, after which the latter is named. On the mainland they mostly feed at Loughros Point and only occasionally at Sheskinmore. Whooper swans use the southern end of Kiltoorish Lough for grazing and roosting on the water. Small numbers of whooper swans also occur on Clooney, Sheskinmore and Sandfield Loughs.

A small number of wintering duck such as teal, mallard and tufted duck are also present on these lakes. Migrant waders appear in autumn, especially in the sheltered muddy shores of Gweebarra Bay and inner Loughros More Bay. Commonest are oystercatcher, redshank, dunlin and curlew. On the sandy beaches flocks of sanderling, dunlin and ringed plover feed in the wet sand at the water's edge. At Sheskinmore in winter the visiting birds of prey usually include hen harrier and buzzard and there have been a few sightings of the rare marsh harrier. Occasionally, a short-eared owl, has been seen in the Rossbeg area. This area is also good for wintering finches, especially twite and linnet.

Fish: The marine fish of the area are quite varied. The largest fish in the Atlantic Ocean, the basking shark, is regularly seen off the coast in this area. Smaller sharks, including tope, are sometimes caught at the entrance to Gweebarra estuary and Loughros More Bay. Mackerel are abundant in Loughros More Bay and Gweebarra Bay in late summer. Cod, pollack and grey gurnard are caught around the rocky shores, including some of the islands. Conger eels are frequent, and can be seen scavenging around the pier at Rossbeg. Sand eels also move about in large shoals in the shallow sandy water in the summer. They spawn in soft sand at the mouth of the Gweebarra River. Gobies, blennies, wrasse and other small fish are plentiful in shallow waters and are often 'trapped' in rock pools when the tide goes out.

The Owenea River, just north of Ardara, is one of Donegal's premier salmon rivers. It has maintained a healthy population of salmon, although sea trout have declined in recent years. In the lower two miles of its channel, the river

Cuckoo wrasse *(photo by Nigel Motyer)*

has deep pools alternating with shallow rocky areas. This river has over fifty pools which have been named by anglers. It is a spate river which floods rapidly after a period of heavy rainfall. The Owentocker River, which flows through the town of Ardara, is a very spatey river but it has very few pools to hold fish. The Gweebarra River has a good run of late spring salmon with summer fish from August onwards. Most of the main rivers are popular rod-fishing waters. Other freshwater fish in the rivers include eels and occasional brown trout.

Dragonflies and damselflies: The area around Ardara-Portnoo provides excellent habitat for dragonflies and damselflies. The combination of clean, shallow pools where the larvae can grow unmolested by fish and wetland habitats rich in insects for the predatory adults is just about ideal for dragonflies. Indeed Sheskinmore Lough and the associated wetlands are regarded as the most species-rich site in Donegal and one of the richest sites in the whole of Ireland. The area has been well studied by Brian Nelson of the Ulster Museum.

There have been records so far of 15 species of dragonflies and damselflies. The most frequent species is the common darter – thousands of adults emerge each year from Sheskinmore Lough around the middle of June. The most interesting species at Sheskinmore are the black-tailed skimmer and the small bluetip. The Rosbeg area is the northernmost known breeding site for the black-tailed skimmer in Ireland. The large, sky-blue males can be seen perched on

Small blue tip damselfly (left) and Black-tailed skimmer *(Robert Thompson)*

bare sand or rocks at the edge of water or the open dunes. The small bluetip is much less obvious but, with patience and luck, can be seen in areas of shallow pools in the marsh west of the main lough at Sheskinmore.

The clear ponds among the dunes near Trawmore hold a variety of species including the spring redtail, common bluetip, common spreadwing and common darter. Moorland hawker also breeds regularly in the permanent ponds and spring hawker and variable bluet are found in good numbers throughout the area. The small, very dark, adults of the black darter can be seen in boggy areas and occasionally around the lake in late summer.

Butterflies: The area is particularly good for butterflies because of the relatively unspoilt diverse habitat and positive microclimate. Twenty-seven butterfly species have been recorded in Donegal during the Donegal Butterfly Survey, coordinated by Bob Aldwell since 1998. In this district, 10km square G79 boasts 24 species, which is the highest number recorded for any such 10km square in Donegal. The neighbouring square (G69) has 22 species.

Among the less common species are the dingy skipper, large heath, marsh fritillary and small blue. Other local resident species readily seen include: dark green fritillary, grayling, green hairstreak, silver-washed fritillary and wall brown. The common blue, green-veined white, meadow brown, orange tip, peacock, ringlet, small copper, small heath and small tortoiseshell are widespread

Clockwise from top: Common blue butterfly *(Robert Thompson)*; six spot burnet moth; yellow shell moth *(Robert Thompson)*; silver washed fritillary

throughout the area. The migrants peacock, painted lady and red admiral occur most years and often breed successfully.

The best months for seeing butterflies are usually June and July and, while butterflies appear throughout the area, a number of districts are especially good for observing them. Pride of place goes to Sheskinmore and adjoining Ballinreavy and Trawmore, where the dingy skipper, dark green fritillary, grayling, marsh fritillary, small blue, small copper, small heath and wall brown all occur, some years in large numbers. Among the other good butterfly areas are Rossbeg/Kiltooris, the cliff path west of Portnoo Harbour, the bog road to the south-east of Bonny Glen Wood and adjoining the narrow road running from Pound Lough to Doon Lough. Wet pasture near Dawros House Hotel supports a profusion of green-veined white, small white and orange tip. Small heath butterflies are common on the heathland areas.

Moths: Moths have been studied by Ralph Sheppard and John Cromie (information on the website www.skylark.ie/donegalmoths/). At least 90 species of larger moths are known from Sheskinmore. With its dunes, heath, marsh and machair habitats, this site is generally regarded as the best moth site in the area. Trapping has not been especially concentrated on Sheskinmore itself, and many of the interesting records are from sites in the wider area, including Portnoo and Kiltooris Lough.

Some moths recorded from the area include argent and sable, brown-line bright-eye, chestnut-coloured carpet, juniper pug, marsh oblique-barred, mouse moth, narrow-bordered five-spot burnet, plain wave, pod lover, red carpet, shaded pug, shore wainscot, small elephant hawk-moth, southern wainscot, straw underwing, grey, rustic, shark, uncertain and thyme pug.

Moths and butterflies – or rather their caterpillars – are often specialist feeders, devoted to one particular plant or to a particular niche habitat. So when an area contains such a diversity of habitats – sand dunes, dry and wet machair, fen, scrub woodland, dry heath and rocky coastal habitats – it is also likely to support a rich and diverse variety of moth and butterfly species. Moth trapping and daytime sightings have shown that the Ardara-Portnoo area, and in particular, Sheskinmore, has indeed an abundance of moth species. These include the rare pretty pinion that feeds on eyebright, as well as coastal specialists such as marbled coronet and the shark with its unusual headgear.

Juniper and wild thyme are common on the heathlands, so it is not surprising that we find juniper-feeding specialists such as the juniper pug and chestnut-coloured carpet, as well as the thyme pug. Quite a few of the interesting moth species in this area are in fact day-flying. On a sunny, still, summer day in the dunes, the abundant six-spot burnet is everywhere: yellow shell and wood tiger are easily found, but the narrow-bordered bee hawk-moth and the forester are more elusive, not to mention the very rare narrow-bordered five-spot burnet.

Beetles: The Reverend W.F. Johnson visited Ardara in 1893 and decided that the area was "fairly good" for beetles on account of the varied landscape. He recorded his captures in *the Irish Naturalist* journal, listing 166 species. Many of these are tiny and obscure creatures but some are more conspicuous due to

Ground beetle *Broscus cephalotes* (Roy Anderson)

their size and particular habits. Some colourful species, such as the violet carabus, orange-spotted carabus and a large purple click beetle *Ctenicera cuprea*, can be found rambling about in daylight in peaty areas whilst most beetles are hiding.

On sand hills and on estuary shores Johnson found species of *Dyschirius* and *Bledius*. Both of these beetles excavate tiny burrows in soft soils and are often found together as the former preys on the latter. On damp sand near fresh water, a sand coloured beetle running about is probably *Bembidion pallidipenne*. Searching under flotsam on the beach and dunes should uncover *Broscus cephalotes*, a large and fearsome-looking beetle with enormous jaws. Turning stones on sandy soils will likely uncover *Serica brunnea*, an orangey-brown beetle that feeds on plant roots. A closely related beetle *Euchlora dubia* which has a green head, shoulders and legs was frequently found on sand dunes by Johnson.

Dung beetles also prefer sandy soils. These animals tunnel underneath animal droppings thereby providing chambers with dung on which their grubs develop. One of these is the dor beetle, a very large globular beetle with iridescent blue/black underside that often flies about at dusk making a loud hum. Numerous species of aquatic beetles live in the many pools and lakes of Ardara-Portnoo, including the great diving beetle, the small whirligig, and a reed beetle, *Plateumaris discolor*. In bog pools live several species of small diving beetles that can tolerate and thrive in the acid conditions. The diving beetle *Acilius sulcatus* lives in large pools without fish as its larvae are prone to being eaten as they swim about in schools. There are probably more species of beetles than any other animal group, but their current status is not well known. A list of some of the more distinctive species from this area, compiled by Dr Stephen McCormack, is given at the back of the book.

Molluscs: The wonderful range of habitats in the Ardara-Portnoo area support many land and freshwater snail species. The rare freshwater pearl mussel occurs in the River Owenea, just north of Ardara, although there is no evidence of it breeding here for some years. This species needs unpolluted water with very clean gravels. The tiny Geyer's whorl snail lives in the wet grasslands and fen at Sheskinmore. The substrate of peat and sand combined with a high water table provides ideal conditions for it to survive in large numbers. Both of these species are of international importance as they are quite rare in Europe.

The other species of note in the area is the wry-necked whorl snail. This tiny species lives in the sand dunes of Sheskinmore. Although it can also live in old walls and wooded habitats, it is very rare in Ireland, and this is one of only six sites in Ireland where it is known to be living. A list of the 41 species of non-marine molluscs, recorded in the area by Dr Evelyn Moorkens, is given at the end of this book.

Marine invertebrates: The wide range of substrates, from exposed rocky shores to sheltered mudflats provides habitats for an equally varied selection of marine invertebrates.

Exposed rocky shores are typically covered in barnacles, mussels and limpets. These are all tightly fixed to the rock so that they cannot be washed off by the powerful waves. In slightly less exposed rocky areas, such as the north side of Inishkeel, a rich rock pool fauna is found at low tide. This includes the distinctive

Clockwise from top left: Common cockle; heart urchin; goose barnacles; mussels and barnacles

purple sea urchins, which line up in crevices or hollows which they wear in the rock. Sea anemones, sponges, shrimps and shore crabs are all common occupants of these pools. Small fish such as gobies and blennies are also found here. The edible crab and lobster are caught commercially and landed at the piers in Portnoo and Rossbeg but most are exported. Inishkeel was a good place for catching crab up to the 1970s but few large specimens now remain.

Sandy shores are the habitats for a range of burrowing animals including the cockle, razorshell and heart urchin. The cockle is a favourite prey item of the oystercatcher. A bivalve called the peppery furrow shell, has especially long siphons that allow it to remain buried deep in the sand. A variety of small burrowing amphipods (relatives of the shrimps) are found in clean sand near low water mark. These attract feeding waders such as sanderling and ringed plover.

Here too lives the burrowing heart urchin, which is also known as the sea potato. After a storm, many millions of the fragile, egg-like skeletons of the heart urchin may be washed up on the beach. The strandline is also a good place to search for unusual oceanic creatures such as jellyfish and goose barnacles. In some years millions of a tiny blue jellyfish called by-the-wind sailor, are washed up on these beaches. The common sandhopper lives among stranded seaweed on the upper shoreline, where it provides food for a variety of birds.

Muddy shores may be less easy to walk but they are rich in invertebrate life. A typical burrowing animal is the lugworm, whose coiled casts appear on the surface at low tide. Other common burrowing worms found in such habitats include the ragworm and the catworm. In the surface layers of the mud live large numbers of a tiny gastropod called the laver spire shell. This is an important food item for the wading birds of these shores.

Conservation

A large part of the countryside and coastline in the Ardara-Portnoo area is covered by the European designations, Special Area of Conservation and Special Protection Area. In theory, this should mean that the landscape is protected against the worst forms of damage. However, we should not be complacent. The changes can be subtle and long-term. Creeping development of holiday houses, golf courses, caravan parks, and all of the associated infrastructure, are taking their toll on the natural environment. The quality of water in rivers is linked with the types of discharges from septic tanks, from agricultural land and from forestry activity. Water should be of the highest quality to support such sensitive species as the freshwater pearl mussel. Subtle changes in land use, such as grazing pressure, can significantly alter the type of vegetation growing in a unique area like Sheskinmore Lough. The initial protection of this superb coastal reserve was the result of a real threat of drainage for agriculture in the 1980s. Coastal and inshore areas can be degraded by beach litter, marine pollution and by overfishing of such species as the lobster. The global problems of climate change are already affecting this area as much as anywhere else in Ireland. We are likely to see, in our lifetimes, significant changes in habitats, species and especially in coastal landforms. The growth of dunes and lagoons on Trawmore Strand along with the associated retreat of the high tide line, with dune erosion at Ballinreavy Strand is a good example of significant landscape change occurring within the locality in our lifetimes.

If you want to report a threat or damage to the natural environment in this area, initial contact should be with:

- National Parks and Wildlife Service, Co. Donegal.
  Telephone 087 6468439 or 074 9137090

- Donegal County Council, County House, Lifford, Co. Donegal.
  Telephone 074 9172222

- Northern Regional Fisheries Board, Ballyshannon, Co. Donegal.
  Telephone 071 9851435

- Department of Communications, Marine, and Natural Resources.
  Telephone 01 6782000

- BirdWatch Ireland, Head Office, Co. Wicklow.
  Telephone 01 2812400

The remoteness of this area means that there are few professional staff available to keep a watch on the natural environment. Protection of the landscape and its natural features depends largely on the landowners and users of the area. Local residents, visitors and those who work in the Ardara-Portnoo area can all become guardians of this wonderful landscape. In the words of Frank Mitchell and Michael Ryan *(Reading the Irish Landscape)* "time is running out for some irreplaceable parts of our inheritance from the past, there is not a moment to lose".

Maps

The standard topographical map of the area is Sheet 10 of the Discovery Series, published by the Ordnance Survey of Ireland. The scale is 1:50,000 and contour interval 10 metres. These maps are available in local shops.

Larger scale maps include the scale six-inch to one mile (1:10,560) series. The last edition of this map was published in the 1920s so it is of some historic interest. Earlier editions were published in the 19th century and show the changes in population and land use (The six inch maps are available by mail order from the website: www.osi.ie).

Detailed geological maps of this area are contained in the publication *Geology of South Donegal* (Long and McConnell 1999). This may be obtained from the Geological Survey of Ireland (available by mail order from the website: www.gsi.ie)

Places to Visit

Bonny Glen

This woodland is located between Maas and Clooney just off the R261. It is signposted from Clooney where a minor road leads to the south. Parking is available at the woodland entrance. The best time to see early woodland flowers is April-May. This is also a good time to listen to the early morning birdsong at its best. Pine marten has been recorded here in recent years.

Naran and Inishkeel

The most spectacular beach in the area is the wide sandy shore in front of Naran dunes. At low tide, the sandy tombolo or spit dries out for long enough to allow access on foot to Inishkeel. Park at the public car park near Naran and walk

Inishkeel and Naran Strand with Aranmore Island in the background

out across the sand. Check the local tide times and make sure you are crossing to the island on a falling (not rising) tide. The island has a small cluster of ruined buildings on the eastern end, including two churches and some interesting graveslabs. The rocky platform exposed on the northern side of the island provides abundant rock pools at low tide. The small fields are used in winter by barnacle geese.

Portnoo Shore

The stretch of sea between Portnoo and Inishkeel is a good place for wintering sea ducks. The road near the church is a good high vantage point. Turn down to the coast from the Post Office in Portnoo and park at the top of the pier. Walk to the end of the pier to see the thick kelp beds visible in the deep water to the east. There is a footpath that leads along the top of the shore from Portnoo pier to the west towards Dunmore Head. However, this eventually opens into fields containing livestock and care should be taken to keep dogs on the lead.

Kiltoorish Lough

This shallow sandy lake has a reedy fringe in places but the shore is rocky for most of its perimeter. Take the road from Portnoo to Rossbeg and park in a safe location after about 4km. Walk along a rough track down the east side of the lake for best views. There is a small ruined clachan (or cluster of cottages) about half way along this track. The woodland at the northern end of the lake is not accessible but can be viewed from the track. The road from Rosbeg to Trawmore passes the southern end of the lake, which is a good place to see feeding herons, ducks and occasionally whooper swans in winter.

Dawros Head

This is the most westerly point of the mainland in this area. From Portnoo, take the road to Rossbeg and turn off at the Dawros Bay Hotel. Follow this minor road for about 2km to where it ends at two metal gates. From here there are footpaths which lead to the north and south coasts of the headland. Beware of leaving the footpaths as there are numerous boggy hollows and areas of reedswamp which are virtually impassible. The cliffs are higher to the north and give excellent views of Arranmore and the tiny Roaninish.

Trawmore

Nearly a kilometre of unspoilt sandy beach and dunes here form the western edge of the Sheskinmore nature reserve. Follow the road from Rossbeg in an easterly direction and, after 2km, turn right for the caravan park. Park outside the entrance to the caravan park and walk the short sandy track to the beach. The beach is wide and very gently sloping but can be very exposed in windy weather. Walk to the southern end and climb the rocky headland of Carrickalahagh to get a good view along Ballinreavy Strand into Loughros More Bay and the estuary of the Owenea that leads to Ardara.

Dawros Head with Inishbarnog beyond (top); Dune slack at Trawmore (bottom)

Sheskinmore

This magnificent complex of lake, marsh, grassland, sand dunes and rocky outcrops lies to the east of Trawmore beach. Follow the R261 road from Ardara to Portnoo for about 6km, turn left for Rossbeg and travel another 4km to the west. The gateway to the nature reserve is opposite the south end of Kiltoorish Lough where there is limited room for car parking on the roadside. Look out for flocks of finches feeding here on the seeds sown for them near the entrance to the reserve. Follow the footpaths into the reserve but take a compass as there are no signs once you leave the road and it is easy to become lost in the dunes. Avoid the large marsh to the west of the lake as there are very deep pools and drainage ditches here. It is best to observe the area from dry ground as the wet areas are very fragile. There are many paths through the dunes and back out onto the beach at Trawmore.

Lakes south of Portnoo

A number of small rocky lakes are scattered about among the hills to the south of Portnoo. These include Lough Fad, Doon Lough, Lough Birroge, Pound Lough, Summy Lough and many others too small to list. Several minor roads give good views over these lakes. For access to Lough Fad, turn off the R261 road at Kilclooney Church and follow the minor road to Clooney. The well-preserved Doon Fort in the middle of Doon Lough is accessible only by boat, which can be hired locally.

Maghera Strand

The inner part of Loughros Beg Bay dries out at low tide to expose a huge sandy beach. The road which runs along the south side of the bay from Ardara passes a beautiful waterfall at Assernacally. Park at the cluster of houses at Maghera (a small parking fee is charged) and walk through the dunes to reach a line of caves near low water mark. These can be dangerous, especially on a rising tide, and care should be taken. The folding and faulting in the Dalradian rocks is particularly clear to see here. There is a magnificent dune system at the mouth of the bay.

Land use history

In 1821, the Reverend John Barrett, who was Church of Ireland rector of the parish of Inishkeel, wrote of conditions in his area around Ardara and Portnoo, just 34 years before the Great Famine. He wrote: "In farms bordering on the shores, the usual succession of crops is, first, potatoes, followed by barley, then oats or flax. In our very sandy district, rye is grown which answers well. Provisions are generally dearer here than in other parts of Ireland; the cause I conceive to be an over abundant population, bad husbandry, small farms and the great consumption of grain in illicit distillation. Were it not for the importation of provisions from the province of Connaught, this parish would very frequently be in danger of starving. The entire of this parish is interspersed with moors and bogs and I know of no inhabitant one mile distant from fuel. There are neither woods, orchards, nurseries or plantations in this parish, and I know from experience they would all thrive. In the districts bordering on the sea shore, seaweed is almost the only manure used. As to lime, it is never used here. There are two ferries between this parish and Lettermacaward for people only, the cattle must swim. There are only a few small boats. My table is usually supplied with fish such as cod and pollack, taken by a currach, a species of boat composed of wicker work and covered with a horse's skin. Not more than thirty people are employed in fishing and, even that small number are only employed in the summer months when the weather is calm. I have learnt that herring have been, of late years, frequently on this coast, but were not taken for want of nets". This account is given in full in Lochlann McGill's book In Conall's Footsteps (2001).

Further Reading

Browne, J. 2005. *Ireland's Mammals*. Browne Books. Kilcullen.

Burningham, H. 2002. Meso-scale morphological changes in the Loughros More Estuary. *Littoral 2002: The Changing Coast*, EUCC Porto, Portugal. Pp. 265-270

Cabot, D. 1999. *Ireland: A natural history*. HarperCollins. London.

Clarke, W, & Harvey, R. 2003. *Donegal Islands*. Cottage Publications. Donaghdee.

Connolly, J. & Monds, T. 2006. *O Foinse go Farraige: The story of the Gweebarra.* The Allen Library.

Fossitt, J.A. 1994. Late-glacial and Holocene vegetation history of western Donegal, Ireland. *Biology and Environment: Proceedings of the Royal Irish Academy* 94B, 1-31.

Fossitt, J.A. 2000. *A Guide to Habitats in Ireland.* The Heritage Council. Kilkenny.

Hart, H.C. 1898. *The Flora of the County Donegal*. London.

Johnson, W. F. 1893. Coleoptera at Ardara, Co. Donegal. *Irish Naturalist*. 2: 53-55

Long, C. B. and McConnell, B.J. 1999. *Geology of South Donegal*. Geological Survey of Ireland. Dublin

McGill, L. 2001. *In Conall's Footsteps*. 2nd Edition. Brandon Books. Dingle, Co. Kerry.

McKeever, P.J. 1999. *A Story through Time: The formation of the scenic landscape of Ireland (North)*. Landscapes from Stone. Belfast.

Mitchell, F. 1990. *The Way that I Followed*. Country House. Dublin.

Mitchell, F. & Ryan, M. 1997 *Reading the Irish Landscape.* Town House Country House. Dublin

Nairn, R. 2005. *Ireland's Coastline: Exploring its nature and heritage*. Collins Press. Cork.

Nelson, B. & Thompson, R. 2004 *The Natural History of Ireland's Dragonflies.* NMAGNI Ulster Museum. Belfast.

O'Reilly, P. 2006. *Rivers of Ireland: A Flyfisher's Guide*. Merlin Unwin Books. Ludlow.

Praeger, R.L. 1934. *The Botanist in Ireland.* Hodges Figgis. Dublin.

Praeger, R.L. 1937. *The Way that I Went*. Hodges Figgis. Dublin.
Praeger, R.L. 1949. *Some Irish Naturalists*. Dundalgan Press. Dundalk.
Sheppard, L. 1992. *Donegal for All Seasons*. Donegal Democrat. Ballyshannon.
Walsh, D. 2004. *Oileain: A guide to the Irish islands*. Pesda Press. Bangor. Wales.

Nature Field Guides

Brooks, S. 1999. *Field Guide to the Dragonflies and Damselflies of Great Britain and Ireland*. Hook. British Wildlife Publishing.
Cabot, D. 2004. *Irish Birds*. HarperCollins. London.
Cameron, R. & Riley, G. 2003. *Land snails in the British Isles*. Occasional Publication 79. Field Studies Council.
Challinor, H. et al 1999. *A Beginner's Guide to Ireland's Seashore*. Sherkin Island Marine Station. Cork.
Chinery, M. 1973. *A Field Guide to the Insects of Britain and Northern Europe*. Collins. London.
Gibson, R., Hextall, B. and Rogers, A. 2001. *A Photographic Guide to the Sea and Shore Life of Britain and North-west Europe*. Oxford University Press. Oxford.
Harde, K. W. 2000. *A field guide in colour to Beetles*. Silverdale Books. Leicester.
Muus, B.J. and Dahlstrom, P. 1974. *Collins Guide to the Sea Fishes of Britain and North-Western Europe*. Collins. London.
Stace, C.A. 1991. *New Flora of the British Isles*. Cambridge University Press. Cambridge.
Svensson, L., Grant, P., Mullarney, K. and Zetterstrom, D. 1999. *Collins Bird Guide*. HarperCollins. London.
Webb, D.A., Parnell, J. and Doogue, D. 1996. *An Irish Flora* (7th edn). Dundalgan Press. Dundalk.
Wilson, J. and Berrow., S. 2006 *A Guide to the Identification of Whales and Dolphins in Ireland*. IWDG, Kilrush, Co. Clare.

Scientific Names of Species Listed

Plants

(compiled by Ralph Sheppard)

Common name	Scientific name
Ash	*Fraxinus excelsior*
Bearberry	*Arctostaphylos uva-ursi*
Bee Orchid	*Ophrys apifera*
Birch	*Betula pubescens*
Bluebell	*Hyacinthoides non-scripta*
Bogbean	*Menyanthes trifoliata*
Bramble	*Rubus fruticosus agg.*
Bulbous Buttercup	*Ranunculus bulbosa*
Cross-leaved heath	*Erica tetralix*
Dense-flowered Orchid	*Neotinea maculata*
Devil's-bit Scabious	*Succisa pratensis*
Gorse	*Ulex europaeus*
Grass-of-Parnassus	*Parnassia palustris*
Greater Spearwort	*Ranunculus lingua*
Hazel	*Corylus avellana*
Heath Dog-violet	*Viola canina*
Hoary Whitlowgrass	*Draba incana*
Juniper	*Juniperus communis*
Marram Grass	*Ammophila arenaria*
Marsh Helleborine	*Epipactis palustris*
Marsh Orchids	*Dactolyrhiza species*
Meadow Thistle	*Cirsium dissectum*
Oak	*Quercus petraea*
Oraches	*Atriplex species*
Petalwort	*Petallophyllum ralfsii*
Pipewort	*Eriocaulon aquaticum*
Primrose	*Primula vulgaris*
Quillwort	*Isoetes lacustris*
Sea Beet	*Beta maritima*
Sheep's-bit	*Jasione montana*
Slender Naiad	*Najas flexilis*
Sycamore	*Acer pseudoplatanus*
Water Mint	*Mentha aquatica*
Wild Thyme	*Thymus praecox*

ANIMALS

Mammals

Common name	Scientific name
American mink	*Mustela vison*
Badger	*Meles meles*
Bottle-nosed dolphin	*Tursiops truncatus*
Brown rat	*Rattus norvegicus*
Fox	*Vulpes vulpes*
Grey seal	*Halichoerus grypus*
Harbour porpoise	*Phocoena phocoena*
Harbour (common) seal	*Phoca vitulina*
Hedgehog	*Erinaceus europaeus*
Killer whale	*Orcinus orca*
Long-tailed field mouse	*Apodemus sylvaticus*
Minke whale	*Balaenoptera acutorostrata*
Mountain hare	*Lepus timidus hibernicus*
Otter	*Lutra lutra*
Pine martin	*Martes martes*
Pygmy shrew	*Sorex minutus*
Rabbit	*Oryctolagus cuniculus*
Stoat	*Mustela erminea hibernicus*
Striped dolphin	*Stenella coeruleoalba*

Birds

Common name	Scientific name
Arctic tern	*Sterna paradisaea*
Barnacle goose	*Branta leucopsis*
Black guillemot	*Cepphus grylle*
Blackbird	*Turdus merula*
Blue tit	*Parus caeruleus*
Buzzard	*Buteo buteo*
Chaffinch	*Fringilla coelebs*
Chough	*Pyrrhocorax pyrrhocorax*
Common gull	*Larus canus*

Common sandpiper	*Actitis hypoleucos*
Cormorant	*Phalacrocorax carbo*
Corncrake	*Crex crex*
Cuckoo	*Cuculus canorus*
Curlew	*Numenius arquata*
Dunlin	*Calidris alpina*
Eider	*Somateria mollissima*
Fulmar	*Fulmarus glacialis*
Gannet	*Morus bassanus*
Golden eagle	*Aquila chrysaetos*
Great black-backed gull	*Larus marinus*
Great tit	*Parus major*
Greenland white-fronted goose	*Anser albifrons flavirostris*
Grey heron	*Ardea cinerea*
Guillemot	*Uria aalge*
Hen harrier	*Circus cyaneus*
Herring gull	*Larus argentatus*
Kestrel	*Falco tinnunculus*
Lapwing	*Vanellus vanellus*
Linnet	*Carduelis cannabina*
Long-tailed duck	*Clangula hyemalis*
Mallard	*Anas platyrhynchos*
Marsh harrier	*Circus aeruginosus*
Meadow pipit	*Anthus pratensis*
Mute swan	*Cygnus olor*
Oystercatcher	*Haematopus ostralegus*
Peregrine falcon	*Falco peregrinus*
Razorbill	*Alca torda*
Raven	*Corvus corax*
Redshank	*Tringa totanus*
Red-throated diver	*Gavia stellata*
Reed bunting	*Emberiza schoeniclus*
Ringed plover	*Charadrius hiaticula*
Robin	*Erithacus rubecula*
Rock pipit	*Anthus petrosus*
Sanderling	*Calidris alba*
Sedge warbler	*Acrocephalus schoenobaenus*
Shag	*Phalacrocorax aristotelis*
Skylark	*Alauda arvensis*
Snipe	*Gallinago gallinago*
Sparrowhawk	*Accipiter nisus*
Starling	*Sturnus vulgaris*
Stonechat	*Saxicola torquata*
Teal	*Anas crecca*
Tufted duck	*Aythya fuligula*
Twite	*Carduelis flavirostris*
Wheatear	*Oenanthe oenanthe*
Whooper swan	*Cygnus cygnus*
Willow warbler	*Philoscopus trochilus*
Wren	*Troglodytes troglodytes*

Reptiles and Amphibians

Common name	**Scientific name**
Common frog	*Rana temporaria*
Common lizard	*Lacerta vivipara*
Common newt	*Triturus vulgaris*
Leathery turtle	*Dermochelys coriacea*

Fish

Common name	**Scientific name**
Basking shark	*Cetorhinus maximus*
Brown trout	*Salmo trutta fario*
Cod	*Gadus morhua*
Conger eel	*Conger conger*
Dogfish	*Scyliorhinus caniculus*
Eel	*Anguila anguilla*
Grey gurnard	*Eutrigla gurnardus*
Mackerel	*Scomber scombrus*
Pollack	*Pollachius pollachius*
Salmon	*Salmo salar*
Sand eel	*Ammodytes tobianus*
Sea trout	*Salmo trutta trutta*
Tope	*Galeorhinus galeus*
Wrasse	*Labrus*

Terrestrial and Freshwater Molluscs

(compiled by Evelyn Moorkens)

Common name	Scientific name
Flat valve snail	*Valvata cristata*
Jenkin's spire snail	*Potamopyrgus antipodarum*
Herald snail	*Carychium minimum*
Dwarf pond snail	*Galba truncatula*
Marsh pond snail	*Lymnaea fuscus*
Great pond snail	*Lymnaea stagnalis*
Pfeiffer's amber snail	*Oxyloma pfeifferi*
Slippery moss snail	*Cochlicopa lubrica*
Thin pillar snail	*Cochlicopa lubricella*
Column snail	*Columella aspera*
Wry-necked whorl snail	*Vertigo pusilla*
Marsh whorl snail	*Vertigo antivertigo*
Striated whorl snail	*Vertigo substriata*
Common whorl snail	*Vertigo pygmaea*
Geyer's whorl snail	*Vertigo geyeri*
English chrysalis snail	*Leiostyla anglica*
Common chrysalis snail	*Lauria cylindracea*
Ribbed grass snail	*Vallonia costata*
Smooth grass snail	*Vallonia pulchella*
Eccentric grass snail	*Vallonia excentrica*
Dwarf snail	*Punctum pygmaeum*
Large black slug	*Arion ater*
Dusky slug	*Arion subfuscus*
Hedgehog slug	*Arion intermedius*
Rayed glass snail	*Nesovitrea hammonis*
Smooth glass snail	*Aegopinella nitidula*
Cellar snail	*Oxychilus cellarius*
Garlic snail	*Oxychilus alliarius*
Shiny glass snail	*Zonitoides nitidus*
Milky field slug	*Deroceras reticulatum*
Tawny glass snail	*Euconulus praticola*
Wrinkled snail	*Candidula intersecta*
Heath snail	*Helicella itala*
Pointed snail	*Cochlicella acuta*
Strawberry snail	*Trichia striolata*
Brown-lipped snail	*Cepaea nemoralis*
Freshwater pearl mussel	*Margaritifera margaritifera*
Porous-shelled pea mussel	*Pisidium obtusale*
Rosy pea mussel	*Pisidium milium*
Red-crusted pea mussel	*Pisidium personatum*
Caserta pea mussel	*Pisidium casertanum*

Butterflies

(compiled by Bob Aldwell)

Common name	Scientific name
Common blue	*Polyommatus icarus*
Dark green fritillary	*Argynnis aglaia*
Dingy skipper	*Erynnis tages*
Grayling	*Hipparchia semele*
Green hairstreak	*Callophrys rubi*
Green-veined white	*Pieris napi*
Large heath	*Coenonympha tullia*
Marsh fritillary	*Euphydryas aurinia*
Meadow brown	*Maniola jurtina*
Orange tip	*Anthocaris cardamines*
Painted lady	*Vanessa cardui*
Peacock	*Inachis io*
Red admiral	*Vanessa atalanta*
Ringlet	*Aphantopus hyperantus*
Silver-washed fritillary	*Argynnis paphia*
Small blue	*Cupido minimus*
Small copper	*Lycaena phlaeas*
Small heath	*Coenonympha pamphilus*
Small tortoiseshell	*Aglais urticae*
Small white	*Pieris rapae*
Wall brown	*Pararge megera*

Moths

(compiled by John Cromie and Ralph Sheppard)

Rare or localised species, mainly coastal:

Common name	Scientific name
Archer's Dart	*Agrotis vestigialis*
Broad-bordered Yellow Underwing	*Noctua fimbriata*
Chestnut-coloured Carpet	*Thera cognata*
Cloaked Minor	*Mesoligia furuncula*
Juniper Pug	*Eupithecia pusillata*
Lesser Cream Wave	*Scopula immutata*
Lime-speck Pug	*Eupithecia centaureata*
Marbled Coronet	*Hadena confusa*
Mouse Moth	*Amphipyra tragopoginis*
Northern Rustic	*Standfussiana lucernea*
Pod Lover	*Hadena perplexa capsophila*
Shore Wainscot	*Mythimna litoralis*
Rustic	*Hoplodrina blanda*
Shark	*Cucullia umbratica*
Uncertain	*Hoplodrina alsines*
Thyme Pug	*Eupithecia distinctaria*
Willow Beauty	*Peribatodes rhomboidaria*

Rare or localised day-flying species, mainly coastal:

Common name	Scientific name
Argent and Sable	*Rheumaptera hastata*
Galium Carpet	*Epirrhoe galiata*
Hummingbird Hawk-moth	*Macroglossum stellatarum*
Narrow-bordered five-spot	Burnet *Zygaena lonicerae*
Narrow-bordered Bee Hawk-moth	*Hemaris tityus*
Pretty Pinion	*Perizoma blandiata*
Small Elephant Hawk-moth	*Deilephila porcellus*
The Forester	*Adscita statices*
Wood Tiger	*Parasemia plantaginis*
Yellow Shell	*Camptogramma bilineata*

Commoner species to look out for:

Common name	Scientific name
Garden Tiger	*Arctia caja*
Six-spot Burnet	*Zygaena filipendulae*

Dragonflies & Damselflies

(compiled by Brian Nelson, Ulster Museum)

Common name	Scientific name
Common Spreadwing	*Lestes sponsa*
Azure Bluet	*Coenagrion puella*
Variable Bluet	*Coenagrion pulchellum*
Common Bluet	*Enallagma cyathigerum*
Common Bluetip	*Ischnura elegans*
Small Bluetip	*Ischnura pumilio*
Spring Redtail	*Pyrrhosoma nymphula*
Amber-winged Hawker	*Aeshna grandis*
Moorland Hawker	*Aeshna juncea*
Spring Hawker	*Brachytron pratense*
Four-spotted Chaser	*Libellula quadrimaculata*
Blacktailed Skimmer	*Orthetrum cancellatum*
Heathland Skimmer	*Orthetrum coerulescens*
Black Darter	*Sympetrum danae*
Common Darter	*Sympetrum striolatum.*

Beetles

(some distinctive species compiled by Stephen McCormack)

Common name	Scientific name
Violet Carabus	*Carabus problematicus*
Orange spotted Carabus	*Carabus clathratus*
Granulated Carabus	*Carabus granulatus*
A Ground Beetle	*Dyschirius politus*
Small Whiligig	*Gyrinus minutus*

Coppery Elaphrus	*Elaphrus cupreus*
Riverbank Elaphrus	*Elaphrus riparius*
Broad Harpalus	*Harpalus latus*
Shiny Harpalus	*Harpalus aeneus*
Whitle legged beetle	*Paranchus albipes*
A Ground beetle	*Bembidion pallidipenne*
Small Diving beetle	*Stictonectes lepidus*
A Diving beetle	*Hydroporus pubescens*
A Diving beetle	*Acilius sulcatus*
A Rove beetle	*Bledius annae*
A Rove beetle	*Bledius fergussoni*
Sexton beetle	*Nicrophorus investigator*
Sexton beetle	*Nicrophorus vespilloides*
Soldier beetle	*Rhagonycha fulva*
Great Diving beetle	*Dytiscus marginalis*
Dor beetle	*Aphodius fimetarius*
Dung beetle	*Geotrupes stercorarius*
Sexton beetle	*Necrophorus humator*
A Chafer	*Sericea brunnea*
A Chafer	*Euchlora dubia*
A Reed beetle	*Plateumaris discolor*

Marine invertebrates

Common name	**Scientific name**
Banded wedge shell	*Donax vittatus*
Barnacle	*Semibalanus balanoides*
By-the-wind sailor	*Velella velella*
Catworm	*Nephthys caeca*
Common cockle	*Cerastoderma edule*
Common limpet	*Patella vulgata*
Common mussel	*Mytilus edulis*
Goose barnacle	*Lepus anatifera*
Heart urchin	*Echinocardium cordatum*
Laver spire shell	*Hydrobia ulvae*
Lobster	*Homarus gammerus*
Lugworm	*Arenicola marina*
Periwinkle	*Littorina spp.*
Peppery furrow shell	*Scrobicularia plana*
Purple sea urchin	*Paracentrotus lividus*
Ragworm	*Nereis diversicolor*
Razorshell	*Ensis ensis*
Sandhopper	*Talitrus saltator*
Shore crab	*Carcinus maenas*